Living in the matrix

Another Way

Numerology for a new day

BiggyBoo Books

Tizz the Buzz word in books

Living in the matrix

Another Way

Numerology for a new day

By
Ellis C. Taylor

This book reveals radical numerological systems. You will not find them anywhere else. The capital letter values and the timing of events are profound changes from every other book and extant system. They are the fruits of countless hours' development and thorough testing over many years.

First published February 2005

ISBN 978-0-9550417-1-6

Published by
BiggyBoo Books
www.biggyboo.com

Also by Ellis Taylor;
IN THESE SIGNS CONQUER
Revealing the secret signs an Age has obscured
ISBN: 978-0-9556861-0-8

The information in this book contains material of a general nature that is intended to complement, not replace, personal advice from your own physician. The author cannot accept responsibility for any difficulties arising from your failure to seek appropriate advice from your medical practitioner.

Front cover illustration:
'Cathar Portal'
© Neil Hague
www.neilhague.com

Dedications

To my ancestors whose fortitude has enabled our generations to flourish.

To my beautiful mum and my dad for helping to bring me into this wonderful world. I have been blessed by your love and your teachings. Mum, your dynamic enthusiasm for knowledge and your phenomenal abilities have always inspired me. And dad your patience, fairness, quiet wit and dignity will live with me always - as well as the debonairness of course (Well I try).

To my two incredible children and my grand kids I thank you with all my heart for the joy you have given me. I painted a rainbow.

To the mums of my two children. We shared very special moments. Although we didn't travel this whole time together we will always be friends. Thank you both for everything. Didn't we do well!

To my sweetheart, my companion through many a life journey, Your incredible talents are only eclipsed by your beauty and kindness. Always an angel I will cherish our love for ever.

To my exceptional family and so many dear friends whose patience for this wandering spirit is often sorely tested.

You have all given me so much.

I love you all. Thank you.

Ellis

Also from Ellis Taylor:

IN THESE SIGNS CONQUER
Revealing the secret signs an Age has obscured

www.biggyboo.com/signs.html

Living in the matrix
Another Way

Numerology for a new day

About the author

Ellis Taylor is a qualified hypnotherapist, professional numerologist, tarot reader, clairvoyant and psychic. A public speaker and writer he has researched and written on esoteric subjects for many years.

Since September 2000 his popular website www.ellisctaylor.com has become a favourite for intuitively sensitive people who are questioning the implausibility of sanctioned explanations. Besides his profound personal experiences his studies have included hypnotherapy, healing, ancient religions, mythology and history. He is the first to admit that his ideas are unconventional but he says that every idea anyone ever had is a message from the Great Unconscious - the mind of God, if you like. Ideas are pristine instantaneous messages unblemished by intellect at the point of reception. Only when the conscious mind (ego and intellect) gets involved does the inspiration become flawed.

Conventional thinking, he says, is basically just another word for ignorance through terrorist conditioning and hence all human judgements are inept through their blighted vision of the full picture. We are here in human form to gather experiences to paint that ever expanding picture not to follow other people's dictates and wallow in their fear-mongering.

We are all aspects of something so intensely magnificent, so welcoming, so You.

Enjoy what you do, live it. Life's a 'trip' man, a breeze,
and O, what a blessing!

Living in the matrix

Another Way

Numerology for a new day

PREFACE

Counting your blessings

"Count your blessings." I often heard that said by the older folk round our way. Although I can trace my ancestry back to moats and manors, and not that many generations back, I grew up in a working class neighbourhood. It was the 1950s and early 60s. We didn't have much money or bags of possessions but we were wealthy beyond words. There were kids everywhere so we always had plenty of friends. And then just at the end of the road were endless acres of fields, woods and streams. We children were out from dawn till dusk and our parents never needed to worry - well perhaps sometimes. We'd chase rabbits, climb trees, fish in the streams, pinch apples and taunt the local farmers to chase us. More often than not my dog Timmy used to come with us. He was part of the gang. We had so many adventures. The weather never worried us, in winter the icicles were as long as Excalibur and in the summer the thunderstorms were wetter and louder than Trafalgar, and the sun it was so hot your roller skates 'd sink into the tarmac about a second before your face. Every kid had a scraped face and scabby knees. We laughed at plasters. We were warriors. All these things were our blessings but we didn't realise it then and I still didn't until I grew up.

Now my blessings are my children and my grand children, my beautiful sweetheart, my family and friends and still, the most magical of lands, the countryside of the Isles, Albion, 'land of my fathers', and mothers. Our blessings are our life experiences, and they are many and varied. They are what shape and enrich us. Not one of them could be bought for all the money ever minted, even the knocks we have, they're ours, something only we know what it feels like to have. I never did count my blessings when I was a youngster. I didn't know what they were when I was a rag-arsed kid and when I think about it, if I did know there weren't enough numbers to count them.* There still aren't but then I found out that numbers don't just count, like Merlin they cast spells.

Their enchanting powers are eternal and irresistible. We never learnt about these things at school. Numbers were for tests Their enchanting powers are eternal and irresistible. We never learnt about these things at school. Numbers were for tests and the only spells they elicited were in the corner of the class room. Sometimes their monotony got you a trip to the headmaster's office for a closer view of the floor and a resulting backside that you couldn't sit down on for half an hour.* If only I had been shown then just how magical numbers really are. This revelation wasn't to come for another 28 years after I left school. I was decorating a lady's house when she started telling me about numerology. She lent me a couple of books and I became fascinated. There began a voyage into a land where numbers whispered secrets and told of things that would come to pass. That was ten years ago and not a day has passed when I haven't studied or woven the mysterious tapestry of numbers. Indeed I now know there are enough numbers to count our blessings. We just have to know how.

Mankind has called upon 'the Science of Numbers' (better known perhaps as *numerology*) for thousands of years. It is an invaluable and accurate technique by which the numerical values of letters and dates are interpreted to reveal the motivations behind characters and events. The term numerology was coined in the 19th century from the Latin word 'numerus', meaning 'number' and the Greek word 'logos', meaning 'word', 'thought' or 'expression'. Throughout the ages it has evolved into several disparate versions according to cultural conditions. And it will keep on changing driven by the same criteria. It seems that English will inevitably become the world language, and along with its inexorable march the cultural influences that have shaped its character. It is now a compulsory language even in Chinese schools. Numerology is truly a science of the moment and will naturally attune to the most prevalent thought patterns. The inevitable result of this is that English numerology will become the world's most used system. But during my studies I realised that English numerology had ceased to be a science in the real sense of the term, and had become a doctrine, and a flawed one at that. Hence this book.

This book is designed for both the professional counsellor and the interested amateur. There is nothing in here that cannot be mastered by anyone who can add numbers together. Practice will make perfect; it really is very simple once you've used the techniques and interpretations a few times. Throughout I've included simple and clear step-by-step procedures using a well-known personality as an example (thanks Mr Parsons,...er Blair).

After a very short while you will be automatically assessing every name, date and circumstance you encounter, such is the passion this subject engenders. And it's fun. You will astound people with your ability to accurately describe them, especially when it's the first time that you ever clapped eyes on each other. And it's useful too. Learn how to assess the best careers, avoid illness and strengthen your immune system. Choose the best colours for the right occasions and environments. Use it for business meetings, contracts and interviews to assess the right times and the characters you will be dealing with.

Like the matrix the possibilities are endless.
There is always another way.

Ellis Taylor
8th February 2005

- I'd better qualify this - you know what mums are like - It was while I was out that I inexplicably became a rag-arsed kid. Mum always dressed us beautifully. That all right mum?

What is the matrix?

The matrix is a 'natural' progressively motivated ever-expanding, and for the most part unpredictable experiential system without which there could not be this experience we call 'life'. Every aspect of creation (and destruction) moves in the matrix indeed WE and EVERYTHING ELSE are the matrix. Every thought, deed and action perpetually creates, destroys, magnifies, copies, expands and intensifies, knits, splits, cuts and tangles the threads of this, the greatest of all tapestries. It is multidimensional, infinite in every way, and because it operates on innumerable planes at the same time a thing is either obvious or invisible according to the position, orientation or viewpoint of the participant in each particular weave of this continuously shifting, ever-evolving and revolving web.

Every aspect of creation (and destruction) moves in the matrix. You live, and you love. To live is an individual duty or mission and is symbolised by the letter 'i' - a letter designed to show a manifested individual (apparently) cut off from its origins (the dot in the 'heavens').

Acknowledging and then understanding the matrix are vital steps towards self-empowerment.

CHAPTER 1

The Letters

"All the world's a stage,
And all the men and women merely players:
They have their exits and their entrances;
And one man in his time plays many parts,"

Numerology is a psychological assessment tool whose accuracy relies upon a multitude of idiosyncrasies which have been embedded in our unconscious by repetitive programming and reinforced every moment of every day. The process begins upon conception and accelerates once we begin school. At the same time that we learn about letters and numbers we are *sentenced* to abide by strict systems of number, word and sentence structure. This compulsory process called *education* becomes a fluent artificer of our unconscious thought patterns and resulting actions.

One fundamental we learn is that every name must be constructed with a string of small letters led by a capital letter. There are some exceptions permitted, when names are entirely written with capitals and when a surname is prefixed with 'de' for instance followed by the second part of the surname which does begin with a capital. But you'll notice that these exceptions elicit brief but strange psychological responses when they are encountered, as will capital and small letters appearing in unconventional circumstances. They are not getting with the programme. Pedants get very upset by this. People with what's called dyslexia or those who have other difficulties with spelling - are not *falling under the spell* - meet extreme prejudice so much so that their whole life can be blighted by those who are. One of the biggest tragedies is that the un-entranced are very often amongst the most imaginative and creative people on this planet.

We do not choose our names, and very rarely do our parents even if they think they did. It is nearly all down to subconscious programming motivating people to choose a name with an energetic pattern that suits their deepest desires for what they want their child to be like. And it's the same with nicknames, they are given to us by others who have an unconscious desire to change us into what they want us to be. And we will change, for better or worse. That sagacious old scribe certainly knew his stuff:

> "Be not afraid of greatness: some are born great, some achieve greatness and some have greatness thrust upon them".
>
> Twelfth Night - Act II, Scene V

Like he says, don't be afraid. You can always change your name anyway.

Everywhere imposed, though not unanimously agreed, structures control human life. Amongst them are the ways that we formulate our communications with each other. We are taught that there are 26 letters in the alphabet and learn them so thoroughly that we can recite them in '*alphabetical order*' at will. We can all see that there are 26 letters A – Z. But what about the small letters a-z? Are these not letter-symbols with their own characteristics too? Granted they sound the same but they don't look the same when we read or *serve a sentence.* Sound is only one of the frequencies that our minds interpret. What about our sight and other perceptive abilities?

In the higher orders of the most secret schools this has all been known for a long time because it was they who designed alphabets in the first place.

With a 52-letter alphabet numerological assessment inevitably becomes more refined and therefore more accurate than any 26 letter system. This first book introduces the reader to the most accurate numerological system available today.

Evaluating the letters

Small letters' values:
The double digits are next reduced to single numbers.

a	b	c	d	e	f	g	h	i	j	k*	l	m
1	2	3	4	5	6	7	8	9	10	11	12	13

n	o	p	q	r	s	t	u	v*	w	x	y	z
14	15	16	17	18	19	20	21	22	23	24	25	26

The revised small letter chart looks like this:

a	b	c	d	e	f	g	h	i	j	k*	l	m
1	2	3	4	5	6	7	8	9	10	11	12	13
									1	2	3	4

n	o	p	q	r	s	t	u	v*	w	x	y	z
14	15	16	17	18	19	20	21	22	23	24	25	26
5	6	7	8	9	10	2	3	4	5	6	7	8
					1							

1	2	3	4	5	6	7	8	9
a	b	c	d	e	f	g	h	i
j	k*	l	m	n	o	p	q	r
s	t	u	v*	w	x	y	z	

•Letters k (11th) and v (22nd) are letters with master number vibrations and require special attention.

continue

Capital letters' values:

*For the purposes of this book capital letters retain their full numerical value.

A	B	C*	D	E	F	G*	H	I	J	K	L*	M
27	28	29	30	31	32	33	34	35	36	37	38	39

N	O	P	Q	R*	S	T	U*	V	W	X	Y	Z
40	41	42	43	44	45	46	47	48	49	50	51	52

So these are the 52 written symbols representing sounds which generate prescribed thought patterns. Our 3rd dimensional environment naturally attunes to number 9. This gives 9 numbers (and zero) revolving into infinity and the first 52 of them are ascribed to the alphabet we learn by rote during school.

Master letters.

In numerology there are certain numbers that require additional attention; these are termed *master numbers*. Master numbers are repeated digits, for instance two ones -11. From the numerical Interpretations of the alphabets we can see that the letters k, v, G and R have master number values.

k = 11
v = 22
G = 33
R = 44

Less easily spotted is that the letters C, L and U are also master numbers when their components are added.

C = 29 (2 + 9) = 11
L = 38 (3 + 8) = 11
U = 47 (4 + 7) = 11

C represents the 29th day of the moon drawn in that aspect. L represents controlled energy circulation, remember the £ sign and the Lira, the Italian currency, which I doubt is an accident because the Roman church designed the alphabet.

U represents a receptacle for liquid, actually blood and semen, the womb and is a secret symbol of the grail.

All of our number and letter symbols are cleverly designed to surreptitiously elicit thought patterns. It really is magic, so no wonder we call the articulation of every letter in a word 'spelling'! Much of the symbolism is graphic sexual symbolism, letter '**a**' for instance, is designed to represent the flaccid male genitals in profile.

And have a look at letter G. Its value is 33. In Freemasonry there are 33 degrees, is this what the mysterious letter G on their insignia stands for? And of course what number 33 represents and manifests.

By now, if you have studied anything to do with religious and secret society symbolism you will probably be noticing patterns emerging.

CHAPTER 2

The Numbers

Like a letter **'a'**, number 1 represents a male creative (generating—generative) symbol - but this time appearing to be active until you notice it is missing some vital wherewithal. The intention of this design is to suggest that every male needs a female partner in order to create. And of course vice-versa) All of the numbers and letters were designed under the auspices of religious schools using similar allegory. My books will decipher and explain these designs.

Each letter and number, due to the intent in their design promotes thoughts akin to what their designs represent in part and in series. This is why numerology cannot fail to work and also how people's minds can be influenced against their will or conscience.

One cannot ascertain through numerology the moral orientation of a subject but numerology does expose potential dispositions. Morals are produced through social conditioning and not an inherent aspect of any soul.

Numerology has tremendous scope for life and vocational guidance, criminal profiling and many other areas of psychological assessment yet its worth continues to be overlooked mainly due to pressure from those who see personal power in this knowledge.

Numerology reveals the unique unconscious aspects and drives of frequencies, which are symbolised by numbers and these are listed under each number below. These numbers constantly urge their subjects to accommodate these requirements. They are driving forces behind every one and every thing's experiences attracting people and circumstances to create increasing avenues on their insatiable quest for unity. Each number holds many permutations of positive and negative and an ambivalent, assertive and passive expression of its unique nature at varying degrees.

However no subject is ever motivated by just one number. Names have more than one letter and subjects usually more than one name. There are other considerations too, including foundation and birth dates, addresses and in fact everywhere a number appears in your life.

Sometimes people concentrate upon a matter to the exclusion of others. This is focussing on the energetic aspect of one particular number, which although on one hand may seem beneficial, always causes problems through their lack of attention to their other numbers' requirements. This imbalance frequently develops difficulties in relationships, health and finances for example. Every number is as powerful as every other and demands equal respect and attention.

When a person realises their ingrained strengths and weaknesses they are powerfully equipped to create a lifestyle they will find fulfilling. We all so deserve the means to do this.

Enter the science of numbers. Refusing to march to the beat of dogma numbers attune with the rhythms of nature itself. They have no conscience or dilemmas over good, bad or indifferent, they just are. Numbers describe elements of energy and energy patterns or frequencies they are not the actual energy itself. Every number has both a cipher (potential) and number 1 (drive) in its makeup. Without the potential there would be no necessity for number 1 and without number 1 the cipher would be pointless. Every number after these is a combination of these two forming relationships to produce varieties of experiences. Understanding this elemental process is a fundamental stage in controlling thought patterns. If you align a number sequence to something then you will automatically harness the natural proclivities of nature which always abides by numbers. Design a set of symbols and give them an ordained numerical sequence, enforce this by repetition or homily and their unconscious directives will unerringly hit their target. Every arm of the human control octopus uses this technique. As I mentioned earlier the most potent form of mind control are the various alphabets and their letters. Why do you think the much vaunted 'education of the people' policies were allowed to go ahead? What happens really when missionaries front up and educate the people? Why do you think that controversial writers live to tell their tales? It's because wittingly and unwittingly, by the very act of communicating they are enforcing the hierarchal sanctioned programming, which is occurring as you read, view or listen to their messages. It's happening right now! But when a secret is exposed it loses its power. Automatically the intellect, unconscious mind and the Great Unconscious is reconnected and instantly you are one with truth. At that moment you are immensely powerful, unconquerable, and full-spirited. What happens after that depends upon your prior social conditioning and your ingrained integrity. But that secret can never hold you in the same grip again – unless you allow it to.

We need to get used to the fact that those who have a vested interest in maintaining their status will use any and many means to retain it. The last thing they want is for people to realise that they don't need them. They have been marauding, using and imposing their will on every human being over countless centuries. These people, institutions and corporations are not our friends. Today many humans are not even a shadow of their real selves relying totally upon intellectual (conscious-physical mind) satisfaction. Like a mouse caught in the gaze of the adder humans are utterly entranced. Intellect has absolutely no talent for discerning reality. Virtually all it can do in its present conditioned state is recognise what it has been told through physical domain interactions and behave according to these. Kept entertained or frightened it enlists the emotional mind to deny the wisdom of our abandoned unconscious proclivities, intuition and imagination. Intuition is not the same as instinct. Instinct sits with and just in front of, the intellect it is responsible for our physical well being and genetic responsibilities. Intuition guides our primary purpose: that of fulfilling our spiritual enlightenment through our physical experiences in order to perpetually refine and expand the Universal Consciousness – god if you like.

Imagination is the process by which we access *god's* picture library accumulated since time began. It and intuition are only available when the intellect is set aside. We've got to dodge past this bouncer on the door and join the party going on in the mansions of our minds to have any chance to understand what our lives are really about. Anything that encourages contemplation and meditation will help; the more frowned on by your intellect and the management, the better. Appreciating the secret power of numbers is the perfect catalyst for bemusing their blundering behemoth.

Mind works

Below is a two-dimensional diagram of a multi-dimensional concept. I designed it for a much larger volume I am currently writing together with a full explanation. I include it here to illustrate how our realms of existence and experience are supposed to work together.

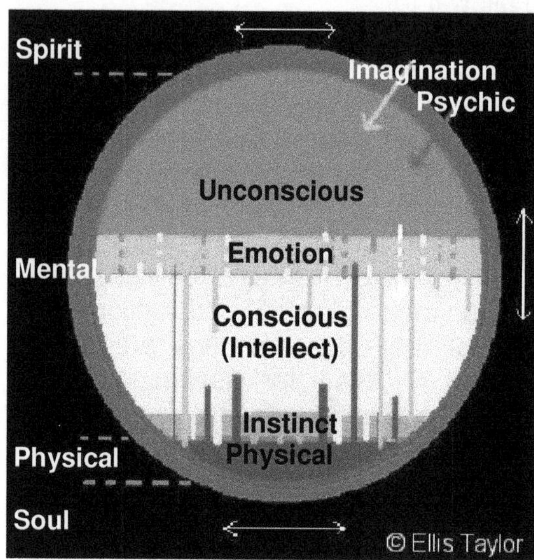

The Realm of Spirit. This is the super conscious, the mind of God, the (Great **S**) Spirit, as opposed to the (Little **s**) spirit. Only our soul has access to the Spirit realm.

The Mental realm, which consists of our unconscious mind, our emotions, the conscious mind and instinct. Only the unconscious mind has access to the soul.

The Physical realm, which is the realm of physical manifestation.

The Soul realm which is the conduit or agent of the Spirit – the messenger that passes information from our unconscious mind to Spirit.

Number interpretation

There are a great deal more words in the name descriptions than you'll usually encounter in numerology books. This is so that the reader can get a better feel for each number's overall character. Although each person is attuned to every aspect of their number whether they enact or show them depends upon their social conditioning and the prevalent circumstances. Everyone, in their hearts will recognise their personal propensities, whether they manifest them or not. During the life cycles (described later) you will notice that every entity temporarily comes under the spell of every number. At these times they will have dealings with, think about or display the characteristics these numbers describe. These visiting numbers may be people, jobs, occasions, places, books, All manner of things. Just because a person holds a number with a particularly nasty trait in its negative aspect this does not mean that the person indulges in these actions. It may mean that they experience it through others or that their job involves interaction with it in some other way - they may be counsellors or investigators, writers even. But in some way this characteristic will show up.

Health

Health problems arise when personal frequencies are abused or neglected. I have included some of the principle health issues of each number, not so that people can go off and worry but so that they can be aware of how these ailments manifest. If you are ill visit your physician but this also enables you to investigate where the appropriate number appears in your chart for an indication of what part of your life is seeking attention.

Colours

Colours are also frequency patterns. The appropriate use of colours in your dress and environment will enhance your life experiences. The colours appropriate to each number and aspect follow the number descriptions.

Vocational opportunities.

Included are just a few suggestions regarding vocational opportunities that harmonise with each number. For brevity in this edition I have concentrated mainly on broad areas of opportunity. If you feel that the word descriptions of the number frequencies fit your sense of a job possibility then consider it.

Well known personality and character examples follow each number. In the main I have used their public names for this book. These are only examples, their potentials are more fully revealed through examining all of their names. In the case of people whose most often used language is not English the letter values will have a coding pertaining to their 'alphabet' system.

Traits of the numbers in alphabetical order:

Zero 0 The unfathomable

Zero is employed as a demarcation point for every new cycle of numbers (experiences) from 1 to 9 within a decade. The numbers 10, 20 and so on are more than the next number after 9 or 19 or whatever, they represent all nine numbers within their domain e.g. 11 to 19 and 21 to 29 etc. This all-encompassing nature makes it the wisest of all the numbers within a decade, yet at the same time it is the most naive. It describes the unknowing about to start out and the all-knowing who has completed the journey. But then the journey is never completed because after one decade a new cycle begins. The wise man is compelled to become the fool again. This wonderful ego-trouncing truth is depicted in the Tarot Fool, card zero.

Bear in mind that in truth, the cipher, although really not a number, precedes every number. We each have this power influencing our lives all of the time.

A zero after a number indicates that deep thinking, contemplation, meditation, spiritual understanding and a holistic approach will be of great benefit. People with a prominent zero in their numbers are apt to daydream when they are in situations they find dull. Zero also represents dimensions, other worlds and also between worlds. When people have a zero in their Secret Self, Life Path or Fate total number, they will have memorable interactions or dealings of one sort or another with these. If they also have a number 16 in the foregoing sectors their experiences will occasionally be sudden and dramatic.

Abeyance, accomplishment, accumulation, alone, assimilation, benefits from a holistic approach, bound, censor, circulation, closed-mind, collection, congregation, contemplation, control, cycles, day-dreams, deep thought, drifting, empty, encompassing, everything, failure, faith, free, full, group, hidden influence, intense, intent, knowing, loss, macrocosm, meditation, microcosm, mind, mystery, naivety, nothing, open mind, possession, potential, secrecy, security, self-control, society, societies, space, spirit, thought, unconscious, unity, victory, viruses, vision, wayward, wisdom.
Letters associated with zero are: j, s, t, B, D, K, N, T and X

Number 1 Self

Action, adventure, aggression, alone, always right, ambition, annoying, assertion, beginnings, blunt, bossy, controlling, courage, cynical, daring, deceitful, determination, direct, discrimination, disorganised, doesn't have to struggle too much opportunities come its way, dogmatism, domineering, easily bored, easily distracted, eccentricity, egotism, essence, exclusive. Has hard but fortifying experiences as a child - usually from or through a male. First, forceful, ideas, incisive, independent, individual, initial, inspired, intelligent, introspective, invention, lazy, leadership, mercenary, mind, needs constant stimulation, needs new experiences, fails to finish what it starts, only self matters, opinionated, opportunity, optimistic, original, own way, pioneer, potential, prevarication, projection, right place right time, schemes, seeks selfish pleasure, sarcastic, selective, self aware, self-consciousness, selfish, self-pity, sharp, shy, singular, slow, sociable, spite, spoilt, straight, stubborn, sullen, superficial, thought, thoughtlessness, unpractical, untidy, vacillation, winner. Male energy.

Letters: a, j, s, B, K, T

Colours:

Secret Self: Aquamarine, black, bronze, brown, buff, cerise, copper, emerald, green, heliotrope, lavender, leather, lilac, maroon, olive, orange, raspberry, rose, ruby, smoke, tan, turquoise, violet.

Persona: Black, cherry, emerald, heliotrope, opal, pearl, raspberry, mustard, rose, ruby, turquoise.

Fate: Aquamarine, amber, apricot, black, blood, cerise, coffee, copper, emerald, flame, gold, henna, lilac maroon, mustard, prune, ruby, russet, salmon, silver, turquoise, violet, white, wisteria, yellow.

Health: Mainly in the head area.

Vocations:

Designer, education, fashion, inventor, investigation, journalism, media, mental health, power and utility industries, research, science, self-employed, sport, travel, writing. Dislikes repetition. Prefers changes in working environment. Best in occupations where it can make use of its talent for new ideas.

Character examples:

Secret Self:	John Pilger
Persona:	Stephen Hawking
Fate:	Eleanor Roosevelt
Life Path:	Martin Luther King 15 Jan 1929 (55)
Pulse:	Nikola Tesla 10 July 1856

Number 2 Cooperation

Accessory, adaptable, arbitration, attractive, balanced, blocking, blunting, calm, caring, careless, changeable, charming, compromise, confused, cooperation, crescent, critical, curved, deceptive, destructive, devotion, devious, diplomatic, dishonest, distracting, divisive, doormat, easily intimidated, elegant, emotional, extreme, faultfinding, fearful, gullible, harmonious, helpful, imitation, impeding, indecisive, interfering, lunar, meddling, modest, moody, negative, over-sensitive, paranoid, partner, passive, peaceful, placating, receptive, reflective, reliable, repetitive, resonate, secretive, self-deprecating, sensitive, sly, spiteful, strident, subordinate, supportive, tactful, tactless, tantrum, tense, timid, tranquillity, unassuming, unavoidable, vacillating, vengeful, victim. Feminine energy.

Many number 2's are also number 11.

Letters: b, k, t, C, L, U

Colours:

Secret Self: Aquamarine, bronze, brown, copper, emerald, heliotrope, ivory, lavender, leather, mustard, olive, rose, smoke, violet, white.

Persona: Brick, bronze, cerise, cherry, claret, emerald, heliotrope, leather, mustard, red, ruby, russet, salmon, turquoise.

Fate: Apricot, black, bronze, buff, coffee, emerald, gold, green, heliotrope, henna, indigo, leather, maroon, mustard, prune, raspberry, salmon, scarlet, violet, white, yellow.

Health: Fluids of the body, blood, waterworks etc, female organs. Parts we have two of e.g. eyes.

Vocations:

Assistants, beauty, carers, entertainment, fashion, health, home, hospitality, librarians, music, receptionists, secretaries, service, welfare.

Character examples:

Secret Self:	James Whale
Persona:	Tom Hanks (11), Michael Jackson (11)
Fate:	Fidel Castro (11)
Life Path:	Edward Woodward 1 June 1930 (11)
Pulse:	Cathy Freeman 16 February 1973 (11)

Number 3 Enlightener

Acquisitive, activity, adaptable, affected, animals, artistic, attention-seeking, avoids emotional confrontation, boastful, busy, charming, cheerful, childish, children and young people, cheat, choice, confident, conjecture, convincing, crafty, deceptive, deluded, demanding, dependent, difficulty with practicalities, disloyal, distracting, draining, duplicity, easily led, effusive, elderly, emotionally vulnerable, energetic, enjoys company of very young and the elderly, entertaining, enthusiastic, envious, excessive, expression, extravagant, false, fanciful, flattering, fleeces, flighty, flirtatious, fortunate, fraud, gift with words, goading, gossip, hasty, healing, hypocrite, hypothetical, imagination, impatient, impeding, impersonal, impulsive, inconsiderate, indecisive, inspired ideas go unrecognised or unused, interfering, introspective, joining, joints, joy, lacks concentration, lethargic, liar, light-fingered, loud, mental, meretricious, mind, missed opportunities, mobility, money, moody, need, not natural manual labourers, over talkative, passionate, persuasive, possibilities, presumptive, pretence, psychology, quack, quick, scattered, self-expression, sensitive to distress, showy, slow, sociable, speech, speed, stands out as a child, sugary, superficial, suspicious, sweet tooth, swindler, tawdry, tease, thief, things taken into the mouth, transformation, unbalanced, unreasoned, unreasonable, unrestrained, untrustworthy, vain, versatile, wary, wearing, withdraws in later life, youthful.

Letters: c, l, u, D, M, V

Colours:

Secret Self: Blood, buff, cherry, indigo, orange.

Persona: Amber, apricot, brick, cherry, green, lavender, olive, orange, pink, prune, straw.

Fate: Amber, blood, brick, cherry, heliotrope, henna, lavender, leather, mustard, olive, orange, pearl, pink, purple, raspberry, rose, ruby, russet, salmon, scarlet, turquoise.

Health: Allergies, asthma, breathing apparatus, hands, joints, teeth, throat area.

Vocations:

Aircraft, art, beauty, care (giving and taking energy - sharing energy - especially animals, children and elderly), communications, cook, craft, draughtsperson, entertainment, farming, fashion, health, hospitality, internet, media, music, politics, power, sales, speaker, sport, teacher, technology, travel, writer.

Character examples:

Secret Self:	Alan Greenspan, John Howard, Michael Jackson
Persona:	David Suzuki
Fate:	Morse, Bill Clinton, Peter Pan
Life Path:	Charles Dickens 7 February 1812
Pulse:	Tommy Cooper 19 March 1922

Number 4 Dedication.

Acclimatization in an alien environment, application, basic, blocks, conforming, conspiratorial, constructive, conventional, crude, demands conventional proof, dependable, detail, destruction, denying, devotion, discipline, domain, dull, easily regulated, earthy, earthy sense of humour, exacting, fair, firearms, fixed ideas, fourth dimension, fussy, greedy, grounding, hard working, honest, inhibited, intellectualism, intolerant, isolated, jealous, lacks emotion, lacks empathy and sympathy, lazy, lethargic, limiting, loyal, military, misunderstands what is different, narrow-minded, nourishing, obsessive, obstructive, only accepts what supports its conditioned view, opinionated, organised, patient, pedantic, petty, physical, practical, planner, ponderous, possessive, pragmatic, presumptive, prison, prohibition, protective, reliable, restrictive, retentive, serious, solid, static, steady, stern, stoic, strict, struggle, stuck, supportive, systematic, tenacious, unemotional, unobservant, untidy, vehicles, violent, work, workaholic.

Letters: d, m, v, E, N, W

Colours:

Secret Self: Heliotrope, ivory, maroon, mustard, raspberry, white.
Persona: Amber, bronze, cerise, flame, ivory, leather, mauve, red, russet, salmon, silver, yellow.
Fate: Blue, bronze, canary, coffee, emerald, green, heliotrope, henna, indigo, ivory, leather, lilac, maroon, mauve, mustard, russet, silver.

Health: Bones-especially back, hands, phobias, stomach, hernias, mental problems due to lack of understanding.

Vocations:

Accounts, architect, armed forces, construction, comic, demolition, employment, engineering, hunter, law, mechanics, music, organiser, planner, security, sport, trades.
Prefers order and stability.

Character examples:

Secret Self:	Prince Harry, Mother Teresa (22), Osama bin Laden (22), Sherlock Holmes (22)
Persona:	James Randi (22),
Life Path:	Mike Tyson 30 June 1966 (22) Margaret Thatcher 13 October 1925 (22) Bill Gates 28 October 1955 (22) Dalai Lama 6 July 1935 (22)
Pulse:	Ian McKellen 25 May 1939 (22)

Number 5 Accumulation. Freedom.

Activity, adaptability, advocate, acquisitive, addiction, administration, adventure, avarice, balance, boastful, careless, change, chaos, charity, coordination, cultivates charm, choices, communication, con artist, conventional, critical, curiosity, demanding, disease, disrespectful, dissatisfaction, distracted, elitist, entertaining, erratic, escape, expects from others, experiences, fickle, freedom, greedy, hasty, humour, impatient, impulsive, inconsiderate, increase, indecisive, inquisitive, intellectual, intelligence, interactive, introspective, irresponsible, lacking in application, lacks finish, lacks stamina, law, lawless, lazy, liar, mental agility, mobility, moody, movement, nervousness, non-conformist, over indulges, perversion, physical, plunder, pollution, prison, profit, progressive, promotion, quick thinking, rebel, reckless, refreshing, representative, research, resourceful, restless, sarcastic, security, sharp of speech, snobbishness, sociable, speech, spy, squandering, stores knowledge, stuck, talent for language, tongue tied, too many irons in the fire, toxicity, travel, trickster, truth, unreliable, untrustworthy, versatility, vitriolic, weight, wit.

Letters: e, n, w, F, O, X

Colours:

Secret Self: Aquamarine, coffee, heliotrope, mauve, red, silver, turquoise, yellow.

Persona: Blue, brick, brown, buff, gold, henna, indigo, pink, salmon, scarlet, smoke, violet.

Fate: Apricot, brick, brown, cerise, cherry, claret, heliotrope, magenta, maroon, olive, orange, pink, purple, raspberry, red, scarlet, smoke, turquoise, violet, wisteria.

Health: Addictions, cancer, coordination, disease, heart, mobility, mouth, reproductive organs, stomach disorders, stroke, over-indulgence, unwise diet, weight.

Vocations:

Academia, adviser, armed services, communications, courier, entertainment, finance, food, hospitality, hunter, law, media, politics, sales, sport, travel.

Character examples:

Secret Self:	Queen Elizabeth
Persona:	Osama bin Laden
Life Path:	James Hewitt 17 January 1958
Pulse:	Bernard Montgomery 17 November 1887 (77)

Number 6 Loyalty. Service. Idealism

Absolute, approval, argumentative, belief in the physical whilst dismissing all else, absorbed, artistic, balance, blocked, boring, bully, cannot 'see' outside its cube, care-less, caring, clinging, collects, companionship, complaining, conceited, conforming, conscientious, controlling, conventional, cooking, cricket, critical, cruel, deflates, dependable, detains, domestically demanding, demands appreciation, dictatorial, diligent, domestic, domineering, duty, embellishing, empathy, encourages, fair, falls for flattery, false, family, fixed opinions and beliefs, friendly, friends, food, gardening, gossip, health, hinders, hoards, home loving, honest, horses, humanitarian, idealist, indispensable, insatiable, interfering, jailer, judgemental, justice, kind, lays down the law, love, loves beauty, martyr, miserly, mundane, music, narrow-minded, nervous, nosey, nurturing, obstinate, patronising, pedantic, petty, poise, ponderous, pragmatic, principled, protective, relatives, reliable, religious, responsibility, righteous, rigid, sanctimonious saving, security, self-righteous, self-sacrifice, service, slavery, slovenly, smug, sociable, social, solid, stable, static, stock-taking, stubborn, stuffy, sustenance, tasteful, teacher, tedious, thief, tidy, timid, timing, tyrannical, un-appreciative, unfulfilled, unselfish, untrustworthy, user, vindictive, welfare, well-being, worrier.6 is similar to 9 in many ways. 6 is more material world orientated and concerned. 6 tends to get personally involved, very often too much with others' concerns, frequently to its own detriment.

Letters: f, o, x, G, P, Y

Colours:

Secret Self: Amber, claret, henna, flame, gold, indigo, pearl, scarlet, straw, turquoise, wisteria.
Persona: Amber, brick, bronze, claret, coffee, wisteria.
Fate: Bronze, buff, cherry, claret, heliotrope, henna, leather, mustard, opal, orange, purple, raspberry, rose, ruby, scarlet, turquoise.

Health: A pronounced tendency to worry brings stress-related problems. Breathing, cancer, headaches, heart, hernias, nervous problems, palpitations, premature aging, rashes, shoulders, ulcers.

Vocations:

Any service industry, shops, domestic, entertainment, health, care, environment, farming, hospitality, sport, beauty, art and craft, office work, music, interior design, police, armed services, security.

Character examples:

Secret Self: Philip Klass (33), Cecil Rhodes (33)
Persona: Paul McCartney (33)
Fate: Jack Nicholson
Life Path: Kofi Annan 8 April 1938 (33)
Albert Einstein 14 March 1879 (33)
Christopher Wren 20 October 1632 (33)
Pulse: Nicole (Mary) Kidman 20 June 1967 (Nicole =66)

Number 7 Higher perception

Ahead of its time, alone, aloof, analytical, avoids showing emotion, calculation, cautious, charm of manner, clairvoyant, classical, cold, countryside, cruel, cynical, detached, detection, difficulties in the material world, dignity, discerning, discovery, discriminating, dislikes crowds, dismissive, drugs, easily bored, eccentric, elitist, explosive, health, hidden energy, hidden motives, hides true feelings, furtive, history, intelligence, intense, introspective, inventive, investigative, lacks communication skills, lacks self-confidence, liquids, literature, mean, meditation, misunderstood, mystery, mystical, nature, natural therapies, needs own space, nerves, nostalgic, observation, occult, panoramic view, patience, perfectionist, prefers to teach self, pride, psychic, quiet, religious, remote viewer, research, reserved, resolute sarcastic, sceptical, scientific, secretive, sees beyond, self-control, sensitive, serenity, shrewd, shy, silence, skilful, specialist, spiritual, spiritual understanding, stoical, study, suspicious, teacher, technology, temper, tests and trials, thinker, too trusting, unbending, unpredictable, unreasonable, unsociable, vain, visionary, water, wisdom.

Letters: g, p, y, H, Q, Z

Colours:

Secret Self: Apricot, aquamarine, magenta, opal, salmon, yellow.
Persona: Brick, brown, heliotrope, indigo, lavender, mustard, olive, smoke, tan, white.
Fate: Brick, cherry, gold, indigo, lavender, magenta, olive, pearl, prune, purple, raspberry, russet, salmon, smoke, violet, white, yellow.

Health: Hearing, mind, loneliness, nerves, waterworks.

Vocations:

Academia, anything involving water or liquids, artist, actor, environment, garden design, health, investigator, miner, oil industry, philosopher, poet, psychic, researcher, science, spiritual occupations, technology, writer.

Character examples:

Secret Self:	Rolf Harris, Janis Joplin
Persona:	David Icke,
Fate:	Prince Philip
Life Path:	Germaine Greer 29 January 1939
Pulse:	Kerry Packer 17 December 1937 (22 LP, 66 Fate)

Number 8 Efficiency. Justice

Accounts, accumulation, affected, aggressive, always in positions where it needs to prove itself, ambitious, architect, articulation, authority, balance, bicycles, boastful, bossy, bully, can go round in circles – sometimes achieving, sometimes not, capable, carrier, cause, cause and effect, circuits, fair competition, confident, consideration, construction, control, courage, critical, cruel, cutting, cycles, cyclones, demands conformity, demands recognition, designer, destruction, diet, discipline, discrimination, disorganised, doesn't listen to or respect others, domain, ears, efficiency, energy, energy fields, engines, environment, executive, expansive, extremes, extrovert, eyes, fields, finance, force, fusion, harmony, has an agenda, hearing, horses, immodest, indecision, indispensable, insistent, jealous, judgement, just, justice, karma, know-it-all (but doesn't), lacks compassion, lacks emotion or has extreme emotions – no happy medium, law, limited, limited perception, magnetism, manipulation, material, materialistic, matrix, medium, meets numerous challenges that takes it to the depths and then rockets them to the heights, military, motivated, motorcycles, movement from one state to another (can mean dimensions, places, mind etc), muscles, needs others, nuclear power, one-tracked, order, organisation, planning, possessive, power, pragmatic, prison, production, protective, pushy, rebounding, represses others, responsibility, rockets from confidence to despondency, scheming, security, seeks power, seeks to impress, self-aggrandising, self-centred, self-employed, self-empowerment, self-harm, showy, shrivelled, sinuous, slow, strenuous activity, stress, stretches, strong, strong survival instincts, success, suicide, supervision, supple, surgery, systems, take over, territory, trade, travel, trucks, tyrannical, unity, vehicles, vengeful, vice, vision, wastes time, weave, weight, whirlpools, wind, windbag.

Letters: h, q, z, I, R

Colours:

Secret Self: Blue, russet, prune, purple, turquoise.
Persona: Aquamarine, black, canary, claret, copper, heliotrope, lavender, mauve, purple, raspberry, silver, wisteria.

Fate:	Apricot, aquamarine, bronze, buff, canary, cerise, claret, copper, ivory, lavender, mauve, opal, purple, tan, wisteria.
Health:	Anything cyclical in the body, arteries, bowels, cancer, depression, disease, ears, eyes, heart, joints, premature aging, reproductive system, respiratory system, self-harm, stomach, stress, weight, viruses.

Vocations:

Any business (according to their other numbers) so long as it is in charge. If not it is essential that leadership prospects are likely. Architecture, armed services, construction, communications, courier, delivery, design, diplomat, engineer, entertainment, farming, finance, food, government, health, law, mechanic, media, planning, politics, surgeon, truck driving, supervisor, supply.

Character examples:

Secret Self:	Bob Geldof, Adolph Hitler
Persona:	Winston Churchill, Saddam Hussein
Fate:	Gordon Brown,
Life Path:	Picasso 25 October 1881 (44)
	George Harrison 25 February 1943
Pulse:	Bill Gates 28 October 1955 (44)
	Rupert Murdoch 11 March 1931 (44)
	John Lennon 9 October 1940 (44)
	Ringo Starr 7 July 1940 (44)

Number 9 Compassion. Love.

Accepting, achievement, aimless, air, alone, art, attempts to possess minds, attracts money, bitter, blames others, can go round in circles – sometimes achieving – sometimes not, burdened, can be deeply hurt becoming very distressed when its dream or ideal is compromised or fails to reach up to its high ideals, charitable, childish, compassion, craft, creative, critical, chooses others ethics, depressed, destructive, detached, doesn't value self, dramatic, dreams, durable, ego, endings, environment, evil, falls for flattery, feels victimised, forgiving, frustrated, gathers and distributes information, generous, gift with words, gives up, gracious, gullible, has big opportunities, head in the clouds, holds hurt, humanitarian, idealistic, impersonal attitude, impressionable, impulsive, indecisive, indifferent, information storage, inspired, international, introspective, kind, lacks confidence, lives in the past, lost, loving, loyal, martyr, mind, misses indicators, misuses or doesn't use talents, moody, multi- talented, music, needs own space, new beginnings frequently caused by disruption or trauma, not forthcoming, optimist, perfectionist, pessimist, philanthropic, philosopher, responsible, revelation, romance, ruthless, secretive, seeks approval, selfless, sky, slow at making decisions, space, steady progress to succeed, stubborn, sullen, the moon, thinker, timid, tolerant, transcendence, transformation, trapped, travel, truth, unappreciated, uncontrolled emotion, understanding, unforgiving, unfulfilled, universal, unrealistic, unselfish, used, very emotional, whirlwinds, won't listen to any advice.

9 is similar to 6 in many ways. 9 is more focussed on thought, considering issues before action. It has genuine concern yet is ble to detach from situations easier than a 6. Social conditioning is apt to make 9's feel guilty about this.

Letters: i, r, A, J, S

Colours:

Secret Self: Aquamarine, brick, brown, canary, copper, emerald, indigo, ivory, lavender, mauve, mustard, leather, olive, pink, rose, smoke, violet, white.

Persona: Apricot, blood, cerise, cherry, emerald, henna, lilac, magenta, maroon, mustard, raspberry, red, salmon, scarlet, silver, turquoise, violet.

Fate: Black, brown, canary, cherry, coffee, emerald, gold, heliotrope, henna, indigo, ivory, lavender, leather, maroon, mauve, mustard, olive, orange, prune, purple, raspberry, red, ruby, salmon, scarlet, silver, smoke, straw, turquoise, violet, white, yellow.

Health: Brain, head area, spine, stroke, viruses.

Vocations:

9's are found in all vocations and are very dependent upon their accompanying numbers, however some notable areas of opportunity are: Aircraft, art, care, charity, craft, entertainment, environment, government, hospitality, interior design, international, law, librarian, media, mental health, music, poet, politics, science, shops, sport, storage, technology, welfare, writer.

Character examples:

Secret Self: Nelson Mandela
Persona: Bob Marley, Nikola Tesla (99)
Fate: David Beckham,
Life Path: Camilla Parker-Bowles 17 July 1947
Pulse: Christopher Reeve 25 September 1952

Special note on Number 16

A number that brings sudden, unexpected dramatic events and trauma and is intended to inspire, destroy egos, highlight falsehood, redirect, and increase awareness. Only a fool seeks revenge against it. 16 shows what reality is and it usually comes into play when anyone or thing is following an inappropriate course and refusing to make changes themselves. In some circumstances its mission is to affect large scale or global changes in consciousness, spiritual understanding. Always for the better in the long term but of course ego cannot see that. In the Tarot it is the Lightening Struck Tower, the most mysterious card in the deck and the only one of the Major Arcana whose action comes from outside the scene. The number relates to the 4th dimension, the fourth world, heaven even. True 16 people have always come to enlighten and/or bring about great changes always through causing anxiety in some way. It is their mission and one that cannot be avoided. The angel number.

Letter: p

Character examples:

Secret Self: Florence Nightingale, Freddie Mercury, Tolkein
Persona: Muhammad Ali
Fate: Prince William
Life Path: Princess Diana 1 July 1961,
JFK 29 May 1917,
Freddie Mercury 5 September 1946,
Uri Geller 20 December 1946
Marilyn Monroe 1 June 1926
Montgomery 17 November 1887
Pulse: Lewis Carroll 27 January 1832

Master numbers

Numbers like 11 and 22, which have repeated digits are known in numerology as master numbers. They combine the qualities of both the component number and their sum total. Their unusual pattern reveals a higher frequency and impact upon their holders than the numbers they total and comprise of.

The characteristics of master numbers:

a) Increase the power of the single number vibration from double to infinity.
b) May merge, fracture, collide or negate the power of the single number vibration.
c) All master numbers have an air of detachment.

When considering a master number's meaning mentally add the prefix great, master or significant to understand their full potential. There are other important factors involving master numbers, which will be revealed in the next book.

Health: All master numbers can manifest difficulties with joints and fractures. For all other health issues refer to the associated numbers.

Number 11 Duality. Opportunities.

Accused, an eye for an eye, arteries, attention seeker, bridges, channels, charisma, concurrence, controlled, copy, cultist, cutting, different, distractive, divided, divisive, domination, duality, electricity, elitist, entertainer, eyes, faithful, false, fame, frustrations, judgement, Justice, illumination, illusion, impressed, impressive, lacks discernment, law, light, magnetic, medium, mimic, mirror, mixed messages, mirror, multiplied 1 issues, needs others to confirm self worth, needs support, needy, negation 1 issues, not independent, nuclear power, opposites, passionate, pipes, plagiarism, possessed, publicity, reflection, routes, self-deceptive, self-destruction, self-righteous, separations to do with 1 issues, sham, short fuse, split personality, suppression, taken advantage of, the same, torn, two separate lives, two plus jobs, twin, tyrannical, unfaithful.

Letters: k, C, L, U
Also see: 1 and 2.

Number 22 Master Builder, Master Planner and Great Destroyer, Enhanced sensitivity

A significant achiever though often unrecognised, misunderstood or unappreciated. Acute senses, cataclysm, catalyst, complete, deprived senses, determined, devotion, divine assistance, divine intervention, driven, dynamic, elitist, environment, global, greatest teachers are females, great love, great sensitivity, harbinger, inferiority complex, international, lacks confidence, leader, magician, major construction, major destruction, multiplied (2 issues), negation (2 issues), organisation, separations (2 issues), sense of mission, separation from females and dependents, split loyalties, universal love, visionary, water, wicked. The description Master Builder applies to more than just bricks and mortar, it describes anything from an empire to a significant book, or signals the parent or grand-parent of a wonder child. It means a major instigator of, or in, the production of something of outstanding and lasting significance.

Letter: v
Also see: 2 and 4

Number 33 Communicating higher knowledge. Inspiration.

An inspired (healer, thinker, speaker and writer), cause, change of voice, child abuse, collector, conference, confidence, confused, control, deception, deliberation, denial, diplomacy, discernment, divine mission, divine responsibility, foundations and beliefs tested, has to battle shyness, higher knowledge, high principles, indecisive, interaction with other living energies, lack of confidence, lack of stability, lacks voice, martyr, mental difficulties, mind manipulation, mission, mobility, multiplied 3 issues, inspiration, negation of 3 issues, noise, over dose, possession, propaganda, quiet, remoulding others ideas, resentment, secrecy, separations to do with 3 issues, silence, interactions with other forms of beings, stays young, transcendence, transformation, trickster, vaccination.

Letter: G
Also see: 3 and 6

Number 44 Transformation. Transcendence.

Change to do with state or being, foundations etc. Acceptance, accused, assassination, avalanches, bomb, car crash, control, combat, coups, cruelty, earth change, earthquakes, envy, explosions, gun shot, inconsiderate, invasion, jealousy, karma, lazy, leader, miserly, movement, multiplied 4 issues, negation 4 issues, openness, oppression, over-worked, patsy, powerful, pressure, self-destruction, separations (4 issues), shape shifting, static, subjugation, transcendence, transformation, two plus jobs, violence, workaholic.

Letter: R
Also see: 4 and 8

Number 55 Indefatigable. Profound experience and awareness.

Advancement, adversary, advice, accumulation, adversity, alienation, altercation, alternation, announcer, astute, broadcasting, challenge, chaos, clumsiness, coma, combat, controlling, conversion, crossing, death, deliberation, denial, discovery, disease, elitist, eloquence, emigration, exploration, foolish, guide, illness, international, interpretation, lack of compassion, lack of stability, lazy, lies, life, long distance movement or change of residence, major change, maths, mobility, motivation, multiplied (5 issues), multi-tasking, negation (5 issues), occult, overlook, overpowering, over see, patsy, plague, poison, publicity, research, resolute, separations (5 issues), sharing, speech, profound, spiritual experience, temptation, tests and trials, traveller, truth, union.

Also see 5, 1 and 0

Number 66 Profound responsibility. Commission.

Balance, commission, committed, different, emotionally steady, environmentally aware, faith, false persona, harmony, honesty, pays quickly for infidelity, justice, loyalty, materially focussed, mission, morality, multiplied (6 issues), negation (6 issues), profound responsibility, rhythm, scheming, separation from family, separations (6 issues), split family, talented decorator, two homes, unreliable, untrustworthy.

Also see: 0, 1, 2, 3, and 6.

Number 77 Confirmation.

Abandonment, adviser, aggressive, ambitious, astute, avatar, blabbermouth, confidence, confirmation, denying, higher awareness, holistically focussed, important dreams, environment, loneliness, magician, manifestation, mental health, mentor, misunderstood, moody, multiplied (7 issues), nature, negation (7 issues), prophet, pushy, reconsideration, revelation, sagacious, secretive, sensitive, separations (7 issues), shaman, suppression of truth, stubborn, tidal, transcendent.

Also see: 0, 1, 4, 5, and 7.

Number 88 Exposure of truth. Eternity

Adversity, admission, black and white, combat, control, corruption, deceptive agenda, defiance, difficulties, discernment, drama, eternity, explosive, exposure, exposure of light and dark, extinction, harassment, harmony, hidden power, high maintenance, hoodwinking, incompatibility, infliction by others, initiate, installation by others, marking territory, mirror, money, multiplied (8 issues), music, negation (8 issues), oppression, piano, placement, plague, powerful allies, powerful foes, removal, secret power, separations (8 issues), serves two masters, solitude, status, subdued, take sides, tragedy, timing, triumph, uncontrolled rage.

Also see: 0, 1, 6, 7, 8

Number 99 Assimilation. Ascension.

Ascension, assimilation of the ego into unconscious realm, the broadcasting, circulation, close, conception, confused, consideration, death, delegating, deliberation, delivering, designer, developing, developing love, diffusing, director, dispersing, distant, distributing, encouraging, eternal, everywhere, fate, indecisive, infinite, inner and outer space, just, mentally focussed, lost, microcosm and the macrocosm, multiplied (9 issues), negation (9 issues), nowhere, producer, reception, reincarnation, separations (9 issues), slow to make decisions, source, stubborn, supreme, the void, unassailable, unfathomable.

Also see: 0, 1, 8 and 9

CHAPTER 3

Analysing a name

Transcending the maths

A name always attracts experiences that match the numeric frequencies derived from its constituent letters. The letters of a name therefore indicate the most appropriate experiential opportunities for that subject. Everyone who impacts upon you will match at least one of your numbers and you can tell with numerology what part of your life this meeting is intended to influence. This book will enable you to verify this for yourself. We are all both teaching and learning from each other all of the time through our interactions.

Every one of our names has its own frequency pattern, derived from the individual vibrations of its component letters. When individual names are brought together they create another frequency pattern. The way we use our name combinations will determine what experiences we will attract. For instance Bill Smith will have different experiences to when he is William Smith. This is why people seem to assume different characters in different situations. Everyone is much more complicated than we ever think.

How to cast a numerology chart for a word or name.

For most purposes there are three key aspects to look for in a name.

1) **The Secret Self**: Your motives, known only to your unconscious. This is revealed by adding together the values of the vowels a,e,i,o,u. Other valid letters are 'w' and 'y' when they are used as vowels and any other letters on occasions when they are not pronounced e.g. g, h, w and p. Also, but confusingly I know, are 'gh' and 'ph' when they combine to pronounce 'f', (as in Gough and Philip). *

2) **The Persona:** The cultivated public face you want people to see or what they perceive you to be. This is revealed by the sum of the consonants but only if they are pronounced. Also 'gh' when the two combine to be silent, (as in Baughan).*

3) **Fate:** What is bound to occur according to the motives, actions and Life Path of a subject. The combined sum of all the letter values in a name.

* Letters g, h and p retain their individual values.

How to work out the Secret Self number:

Technique

1) Write out the subject's name.
2) Write out each letter's value above each appropriate letter (refer to the chapter on letter values).
3) Add together the numbers in each name separately until you have a single digit or a master number.
4) Add together the totals of all of the names and keep adding until you have a single digit or master number.

Throughout, Tony Blair is the subject. This is not his real full name, but what is known as his public name. It is treated in exactly the same way. Bear in mind that at all times the several names that people are known by are influencing that subject. The most commonly used one always having the predominant effect.

Subject: Tony Blair

Secret Self

```
                5
      4                 1
     13                10        = 23
   6    7            1  9
 T  o  n  y    B  l  a  i  r
```

The first name, Tony has a value of 13, which when the digits are added together totals 4.

The last name, Blair has a value of 10. We then add 1 + 0 giving us a total of 1.

The full name, 'Tony Blair' has a first total value, or frequency of 23. The ensuing totals are 4 and 1, which result in 5. This is the combined number of his Secret Self frequency.

Secret Self:
Tony: 13/4
Blair: 10/1
Combined Secret Self: 23/5

How to work out the Persona number:

Technique

1) Write out the subject's name.
2) Write out each letter's value under each appropriate letter (refer to the chapter on letter values).
3) Add together the numbers in each name separately until you have a single digit or a master number.
4) Add together the totals of all of the names and keep adding until you have a single digit or master number.

Subject: **Tony Blair**

Persona

T	**o**	**n**	**y**	**B**	**l**	**a**	**i**	**r**
46		5		28	3			9
		51				40		
		6				4		
				10				
				1				

The first name, Tony has a value of 51, the sum of which is 6.

The last name, Blair has a value of 40. We then add 4 + 0 giving us a total of 4.

The full name, Tony Blair has frequency of 91. The separate totals are 6 and 4, which comes to 10. adding 1 + 0 gives a sum of 1. This is the combined number of his Persona frequency.

Persona:
Tony: 51/6
Blair: 40/4
Combined Persona: 91/10/1

How to work out the Fate number:

Technique

1) Write out the subject's name.
2) Write out each letter's value under each appropriate letter (refer to the chapter on letter values).
3) Add together the numbers in each name separately until you have a single digit or a master number.
4) Add together the totals of all of the names and keep adding until you have a single digit or master number.

Subject: **Tony Blair**

Fate

```
 T  o n y   B  l a i r
46  6 5 7  28  3 1 9 9
   64          50
   10           5
    1           5
          6
```

The first name, Tony has a value of 64, which when added together totals 10. Add 1 + 0 to arrive at 1.

The last name, Blair has a value of 50. We then add 5 + 0 giving us a total of 5.

The full name, Tony Blair has a value, or frequency of 114. The separate totals are 1 and 5, which comes to 6. This is the combined number of his Fate frequency.

Fate:
Tony: 64/10/1
Blair: 50/5
Combined Public name Fate: 114/6

Comment:

Tony Blair will present his number 1 personality to the public choosing its most attractive, powerful face. This Persona number is derived 51 and 40; in this sector the numbers can involve in argument, combat, self-seeking and law. However these are slightly disguised by the derived numbers 6 and 4, meaning you're not necessarily going to get what you see. A positive number 6 is honest, responsible, caring and committed to service to the community. A positive number 4 is strong, fair, conventional and trustworthy. A positive number 1 is a leader, courageous, active and innovative. However his Secret Self is a number 5, derived from numbers 4 and 1. Although these two numbers are present in his Persona numbers the Secret Self is more interested in what's best for the subject (according with the 51 and 40 in his Persona). The vibration of number 5 does not sit happily with either 4 or 6. It likes change and the freedom to do what it wants to do. With the number 1 present in this situation this can potentially accentuate the selfish aspects of both 4 and 5 and lead to a deceptive, dictatorial personality.

Tony Blair has had repeated heart problems. Number 5 rules the physical heart and is the number of his Secret Self and the Fate energy of the surname Blair. This suggests that there is something to do with Tony Blair's motivations (Secret Self) causing these health scares. He is defying, ignoring or contravening the positive aspects of his Secret Self (number 5 and the numbers it derives from) and this is impacting the rhythm of his life. That number 5 appears in his Fate numbers suggests what some would call a genetic inheritance – but it's actually encoded in his (non-physical) frequency pattern.

Also within Tony Blair's Persona frequency is the number 91. This number, on the face of it, would show a benign (9) personality (1) intent on leading (1) humanitarian (9) campaigns (1). But, when number 91 is being misrepresented, sudden dramatic, violent or unexpected experiences are guaranteed because it turns into a number 16.

It was another heart attack that brought Tony Blair to the forefront of the Labour Party, and consequently the prime minister-ship. On 12 May 1994 (totals 4 – Tony Secret Self, Blair Persona) John Smith, the then leader of the Labour Party died from a heart attack. John Smith also had a 5 Secret Self.

His Fate number 6 is derived through 1 and 5. In fact if you look at his number pattern throughout the same numbers crop up time and again. Behind the 1 and the 5 are 64 and 50. Together, positively 64 and 50 are seeking stability, strength, responsibility, truth, fairness, freedom and openness. There is a mission to selflessly share and care.

The name 'Tony Blair' includes a number of zeros, three 10s, a 40 and a 50.

Please refer to the chapter on number values for the meanings of Tony Blair's numbers.

CHAPTER 4

The Life Path

Analysing a date

The Life Path is calculated from the numbers of the birth and foundation dates. At your birth a unique pattern of cosmic and earthly energies accompanied your debut as a physically individual human being and the same is true for the foundation of any independent entity or recognised independent presence, be it a nation, a building, business, a discovery or whatever.

Incorporated into the manifesting presence are all of the experiences, and the feelings around them it sensed since conception. On a macrocosmic level, on our level of experience, this melting pot of energetic ingredients attunes to one of 9 major life streams or 'Life Paths', numbered from 1 to 9. Every *Life Path* is itself divided into 9 sub lanes and these sub lanes themselves incorporate 9 sub lanes. This process of individualisation continues on and into infinity. Once a newfound being or entity has aligned with its own path (really a sub path) there it stays until the physical experience is over. The numbers that construct our 'Life Path number' are sub lanes of these sub paths. Other subdivision indicators include the hour, minutes and seconds etc and location at the moment of birth or foundation. All of these paths weave around, forming a constantly-moving, serpentine matrix of energy streams, continually encountering one another and because of their ethereal nature, passing through or along each other.

Each number derived from the letters of names perpetually interacts with the paths but seeks out other paths that match its own frequency pattern numbers. When it succeeds, it naturally passes along that stream, intending to absorb energy from it. At times the other stream actually takes energy from it. These are what we call lessons, part of which is knowing when to get out, or when not to get involved at all. The complexity of experiences are magnified when the subject has master numbers anywhere on their chart as they will be attracting and attracted to the master number vibration as well as the single digit it intensifies. This results in several *Life Paths* to negotiate and an increased variety of potential lessons. Some prefer to tootle along on their single digit vibration. And why not? As with the frequencies of our names, the influences upon our birth times are not something we chose. Every date division number is artificial. Our year numbers, calendar months and the day numbers in them were all invented by the secret schools. But because they have become a fundamental in human consciousness they work in our artificial world.

From the Life Path numbers we ascertain the arenas of activity best suited to the subject's qualities. If you are examining vocational opportunities, for instance, the Life Path is the prime indicator but it is necessary to ensure that the requirements of the name numbers can be satisfied as well. For instance: a number 6 Life Path is suited to nursing but if he or she has prominent 1's and 5's then they are unlikely to be happy if their work demands too much restriction, lacks variety or it means that they have to stay in the same place, which may indicate that a hospital is not the best place for their talents. There are other ways to nurse.

How to calculate the Life Path

Using Mr Blair again as an example let's have a look at what his Life Path has to tell us.

Tony Blair
Born: 6th May 1953

Technique:

1) Convert the month to its number according to its place in the calendar year.

The months are allocated their numbers according to their positions in the solar year like so:

January	1	July	7
February	2	August	8
March	3	September	9
April	4	October	10/1
May	5	November	*11/2
June	6	December	12/3

Note: Notice that November's placing is a master number. Numerology's job is to look for potentials.

First Life Path calculation

2) Write out the day, month and year.
3) Add these numbers together until you get a single digit, making a note of *master numbers*, if there are any.

The result is the first Life Path number.

May = 5

6 5 1953
1964
20
First Life Path number 2

Second Life Path calculation

4) Repeat steps 1 and 2.
5) Reduce the day, month and year numbers to single digits
6) Add these numbers together until you get a single digit, making a note of master numbers, if there are any.

The result is the second Life Path number.

	6	5	1953
	6	5	18
	6	5	9
		20	
Second Life Path number		2	

Third Life Path calculation

7) Repeat steps 1 and 2.
8) Reduce the day, month and year numbers to single digits (if relevant), except the *master numbers.*
9) Add these numbers together until you get a single digit. If you end up with another *master number* mark it, but then reduce it to a single digit.

The result is the third Life Path number.

*Third Life Path number (In this instance) n/a

*In Tony Blair's case there is no *master number* to account for...yet.

Fourth Life Path calculation

10) Repeat steps 1 and 2.
11) Add all of the numbers across until you get a single digit. If another *master number* fronts up mark it, but then reduce it to a single digit. The result is the fourth 'Life Path' number.

	6	5	1953
		29	
Fourth Life Path number		*11	
		2	

Tony Blair has a Life Path of 2 with the higher frequency potential of 11.

So at his birth Tony Blair emerged into the world synchronising with the high frequency 11 and its sum 2. Tony Blair is therefore unable to do anything alone. Again we recognise the same numbers he was dealt when he accepted the name Tony Blair. His master number 11 arrives through number 29 (the same Life Path as Bill Clinton, by the way). This is a number of great love and great loss, the full gamut of emotions. Tony Blair is governed by his emotions and the emotions of others to a great extent. He will also bring these emotional responses to the surface in others. It's up to him whether he evinces happy, fearful or miserable reactions.

In 2004 the Blair's bought a house in London, it was number 29 of all things, 29 Connaught Square. Thereby fulfilling the demands of his Life Path 29/11. There'll be some heartache there.

Refer to the chapter on number values for further insights.

***The third Life Path with a master number**

I noted above that Tony Blair did not have a master number to account for in his third Life Path calculation.

This is how it's done (We'll use his distant cousin in this example, for a change:

Prince Charles
Born 14 November 1948

1) Convert the month to its number according to its place in the calendar year.
2) Write out the day, month and year.
3) Reduce the day, month and year numbers to single digits (if relevant), except the master numbers.
4) Add these numbers together until you get a single digit. If you get another master number mark it, but then reduce it to a single digit.

The result is the third Life Path number.

November = 11

14   11   1948
5   *11   * 22
38
*11
2

Comment: Prince Charles has a master number month (11) and a master number year (22). His total Life Path is also a master number (11), which arrives via number 38, suggesting that there is some karma to be worked out via a child, probably one of his.

Readers may find it interesting to compare Tony Blair's numerology with that of George Walker Bush who was born on 6 July 1946.

CHAPTER 5

The Pulse

There is another frequency that all of us can bring into play to help us through challenging moments. It is not a number that we use, or should use too often, because it magnifies the power of the number's vibration astronomically and may result in a weakened physical and mental system. It seems to simmer behind our other frequency patterns coming into play naturally when circumstances call for it. The Pulse Number joins with the other personal numbers to accelerate whatever it is that the subject is focussing on, rather like adrenalin or the overdrive function in a car. Even though successful people do use this boost energy regularly it doesn't go unnoticed that they seem to succumb to very serious health problems.

Whenever the big tests come along you will find this number involved in the players or the circumstances.

The Pulse Number is calculated by adding together the Fate Number and the Life Path.

Tony Blair's Life Path is 11/2. His Fate Number is 6. Together they total 17/8, which is his Pulse number.

CHAPTER 6

Counting Time

Timing, as they say, is everything.

At the moment of our conception a unique pattern of inter-dimensional, cosmic and earthly forces meet us and accompany us into the physical realm. With these come the genetic blueprints of our ancestors, a sense of purpose, talents, abilities, and a dowry of past life experiences. This is the scrubbed up and polished essential fluttering spark looking for action. On hitting the deck, so to speak, it is immediately bombarded by everything its parents have experienced and everything its mother experiences or comes into contact with after that. For the majority there is at least 9 months' experience of this constant, inescapable alien milieu. Not exactly the stuff that dreams are made of but at least it feels physically secure. Not surprising then that most of us are a pain to eject.

It is not possible for us to know the precise moment of our conception, which is a shame I think, but there you are. Our fleeting moment of perfection ingrained deep within our unconscious drives us to return home but it also understands that there is a purpose, we must attempt to accomplish. Tragically this unconscious wisdom becomes less and less distinct as the clutches of the physical environment inexorably claim our consciousness. In the 'civilised world' we learn that there is nothing other than what our physical senses can perceive. We learn that there is nothing after death and we are taught that the whole of creation and everything that goes on in it is a huge cosmic accident. All lies, and fingers crossed when people have read this book they will realise this; our lives can only be better for it, but first we have to understand what the lies are.

In the succinct words of one of the world's greatest philosophers, wits and sages, a dream traveller and a cosmic-grade initiate of the most secret schools of knowledge:

" There is more to this world Horatio than is ever dreamt of in your philosophy."

Life in our time, I suppose, and we're here to experience it, both glad and sad. But what a blessing!

What we can do is calculate the approximate time we were conceived, well the month anyway. And I suspect that if you get to know your numbers and how the frequencies feel you can get a pretty good idea of the actual date, but that's only a feeling I have because I think, through meditation, I know my time. Another book will look into conception timing. Anyway, left to Mother Nature we are all allocated 9 moons in the womb. And if Mother Nature says a cycle of 9 is appropriate for human beings, then who am I to argue?

The human species is more attuned to the rhythm of the moon, than it is to the sun. The ancients accepted this and regulated their lives accordingly. Our bodies are, for the most part, made up of water, which means that there are tides washing around within all of us. And what controls the tides? The moon. In fact there's a lot of head scratching concerning humans and their discordance with this planet. Why it is that menstruation is governed by lunar influence? Why is it that we have to wear clothes? And why is it that we have to shade our eyes in bright sunlight with a hand or pair of sunglasses? As Reg Presley says, "Cows don't do it." And nor do any other creatures. Are we an alien species to this planet? I think so, and I'm not the only one. Native cultures everywhere insist on it and our ancestors recorded this in documents and tablets that are turning up all over the place.

Anyway, many years ago I realised that to be accurate, every numerological forecast for earth's human beings and their affairs must revolve around the lunar and 3rd dimension number 9. This is supported by the eternal reverence for numbers 3 and 9, which have always been considered magical rhythms of transformation and transcendence. I've designed a simple chart around these numbers, which will enable you to accurately forecast the experiences you will meet in any specific period. You will also be able to look back at certain times in your life and recognise the frequencies motivating those moments.

This book is introducing revolutionary new systems. You will not find them anywhere else. The capital letter values and the timing of events are profound changes to every other book and extant system

They are the fruits of countless hours' development and thorough testing over many years.

As you move through life from one cycle to another you will meet not just the moments that are described by the numbers but the people too. Your best friends, partners and others who you feel a bond with always have mostly the same numbers as you do as likewise do those you don't get along with. Life reflects back at us and every person and every occasion we encounter are amazing designed synchronicities purposely woven into this tapestry we call life.

There are more advanced techniques which I will show you in a future book but let's get to understand the basics. With the system below we will look at the numbers influencing days, months, years and series of 3-year periods. This is the most accurate numerological timing system you will find anywhere today.

The chart is really very simple to set up:

Periodic Pattern chart

MONTHS	1	2	3	4	5	6	7	8	9 ►
(a)									
(b)									
(c)									
(d)									

Draw up a chart like the one above but with as many columns as you wish. (27 columns will fit comfortably across an A4 sheet.)

This chart begins on the same day-number as the actual day of birth.

Setting up the chart

Stage 1:

1) Take the name and date of birth or foundation. Write these down above the chart with the birth day-number below them.

2) Under 'Month' in box (a) write the name of the birth month proceeded by the name of the month 9 months earlier and separate them with a hyphen. In row (a) write down: August-May

3) In box (b) write the name of the month of birth followed by the name of the month 9 months later separated by a hyphen. In row (b) write down May-February

4) In box (c) write down the name of the latter month, in this case February, followed by the month occurring 9 months later. In row (c) write down February-November

5) In box (d) write down the name of the latter month, in this case November, followed by the month occurring 9 months later. In row (d) write down November-August. *

The chart will now look similar to this:

Tony Blair
6 May 1953
Birth day-number: 6

Months	**1**	**2**	**3**	**4**	**5**	**6 ▸**
August - May						
May - February						
February - November						
November - August						

*The last month will always be the same as the first month at the top of the list.

Months	**1**	**2**	**3**	**4**	**5**	**6 ▸**
August - May	(e) 1952-3					
May - February	(f) 1953-4					
February - November	(g) 1954					
November - August	(h) 1954-5					

Stage 2

1) In column number 1 of the table write down the pertinent years. Tony Blair was born in May 1953 so conception occurred within 2 weeks either side of 6th August 1952. The 9-month period crosses from 1952 to 1953. In box (e) write down 1952 – 1953 (or 52 – 53).
2) Continue in the same fashion all the way down the list. You will notice that one of the annual periods consists of a single year. (In Tony Blair's case it is the row beginning with1954.)
3) Continue filling out the chart from top to bottom through the chart until the time you have decided upon.

We have now set up the cycles chart.

Using the chart

M-cycles

A-cycles

Months	1	2	3	4	5	6	7▶
Aug - May	52-53	55-56	58-59	61-62	64-65	67-68	70-71
May - Feb	53-54	56-57	59-60	62-63	65-66	68-69	71-72
Feb - Nov	54	57	60	63	66	69	72
Nov - Aug	54-55	57-58	60-61	63-64	66-67	69-70	72-73

8	9	10	11	12	13	14	15	16	17	18
73-74	76-77	79-80	82-83	85-86	88-89	91-92	94-95	97-98	00-01	03-04
74-75	77-78	80-81	83-84	86-87	89-90	92-93	95-96	98-99	01-02	04-05
75	78	81	84	87	90	93	96	99	02	05
75-76	78-79	81-82	84-85	87-88	90-91	93-94	96-97	99-00	02-03	05-06

The M-cycles: The columns are very important; they each represent a 3-year span. Each column I call the 'M-cycle'. The first column is called the 'M-1' cycle, the second the 'M-2' cycle and so on. Each step can also be deciphered using the same means to discover even tighter time frames.

The A-cycles: One box is a 9-month cycle, called the 'A-cycle'. The first box is called the 'A-1 cycle', the second the 'A-2 cycle' and so forth. They are ascertained according to their numerical position.

The Personal Month cycle: The Personal Month number is the number of the month in the A–cycle.

Example: For Tony Blair 4 August would be Personal Month 9, A-cycle 24 and M-cycle 6.
20 August 1970 would be in Personal Month 1, A-cycle 25 and M-cycle 7.
To interpret the numbers refer to the chapter on number meanings.

Every cycle begins and ends on the birth day-number.

In the next pages we will use the chart to examine some significant events in Tony Blair's life.

Leo Blair senior's stroke on 4th July 1964.
(M-cycle 4. A-cycle 16. Personal Month 8.)

```
  4  7  1964
4  7     20
      31
       4
```

Tony Blair's father, Leo Blair, (real name Leo Parsons), had a devastating stroke at age 42 (6). Tony Blair was 11* years old.

On American Independence Day, 4 July 1964 Leo Blair suffered a stroke.

The M-cycle, day and date number is 4; this can elicit tests and trials, confinement and difficulty. Number 4 is associated with masculine energy, no matter the gender, rest, work, stability, hardship and obstacles. Number 4 is in Tony Blair's Secret Self first name and his Persona surname.

The A-cycle is number 16, a number that can bring just this sort of traumatic event.

The year number is 2, and the day and month total 11/2, denoting blood and arteries. Number 11/2 is his Birth Path number.

The Personal Month number 8, his Pulse number, relates to the illness and this date was right on the cusp of the 9 Personal Month – Tony Blair's Personal Months begin on the 6th of every month. 9 relates to the brain.

Married Cherie Booth on 29th March 1980.
(M-cycle 10. A-cycle 37. Personal Month 8.)

29 3 1980
11* 3 18
11 3 9
23
5

The M-cycle and A-cycle 37 are 10 or 1 (3 + 7 = 10). These numbers are in the Blair surname's Secret Self, the full total of his Persona, his first name's Fate total, and the century number (19/10/1).

The day number 29 and its derivative master number 11 and number 2 are his Life Path numbers.

The Personal Month number 8 is his Pulse number.

The total date numbers 23 and 5 are in Tony Blair's Secret Self and is the Blair surname Fate number.

The year number 9 is his birth year.

Cherie Booth's birth date 23rd September 1954 totals to a 6 Life Path, the same as Tony Blair's birth day, first name Persona and full Fate number. 23 has a sum of 5 and is the same as Tony Blair's Secret Self and Blair Fate number. Cherie totals 11, as does the Booth Persona, the same as Tony Blair's Life Path. Booth totals 5 - see above. As Cherie Blair and Cherie Booth, the Fate totals are the same, 16 or 7.

Gained the seat of Sedgfield on 10 June 1983
(M-cycle 11. A-cycle 42. Personal month 2.)

```
10  6  1983
 1  6   21
 1  6   3
    10
     1
```

The M-cycle 11 and his Personal Month 2 attune with his 'Life Path' number.

The A-Cycle 42, which denotes 6, is his full Fate number and birthday number.

The day and date numbers 10 and 1 appear in his Secret Self surname and his first name's Fate number. They are also the numbers forming his Life Path 11.

Made party leader on 21 July 1994
(M-cycle14. A-cycle 56. Personal Month 9.)

21 7 1994
3 7 23
3 7 5
15
6

The M-cycle 14 derives 5, Tony Blair's full Secret Self total, the Blair name total Fate number and the year number. The numbers 1 and 4 relate too. Number 1 is his Blair Secret Self, Tony Blair Persona and his Tony Fate. Number 4 is his Blair Persona and Tony Secret Self.

The A-cycle 56 denotes 11, his Life Path number. The 5 and 6 in 56 are also prominent. Number 5 is his Tony Blair Secret Self and his Blair Persona. Number 6 is the Tony Persona and Tony Blair's full Fate number.

The Personal Month number 9 signals achievement. This occasion occurred 16 days prior to the cusp period for all of the cycles going into the next M-cycle 15, A-cycle 57 and a Personal Month 1.

Proclaimed Prime Minister on 2 May 1997 (M-cycle 15. A-cycle 60. Personal Month 6).

2 5 1997
2 5 26
2 5 8
15
6

How anyone can think that everything is up to chance and the ballot box I don't know. Anyway, after 18 years of Tory office, galloping over the horizon comes Tony Blair's Labour Party.

The nation flocked to the polls on the 1st when our 'Tone' was in gear on a number 1 day, in a 5 month, a 26 (2 and 6) - 8 year, and a 16 decade (97 = 16). All of these significant numbers doing more for his ambitions than any determined cross on a ballot paper. After midnight the election turned into a pumpkin but no one noticed for a while. The red team was declared the winner and Britain got a new prime minister, working from Number 10 Downing Street but living in Number 11. Although Number 10 matches his ego (Persona) perfectly it seems Number 11 was more conducive to his future plans, being his Fate number. The official reason is that Number 10 was too small for a family man. In the end he took the best of both worlds Number 10 for work and Number 11 for personal life. It certainly was Tony Blair's day again.

His M-cycle 15 totals 6. His A-cycle totals 6. His Personal Month is 6. His *coronation* day number was 6. Number 6 is his Fate number, Tony Persona and birthday number. The numbers 1 and 5 turn up again in the M-cycle and the election day, victory day and month numbers. Number 1 his Blair Secret Self, his Tony Blair Persona and his Tony Fate number. Number 5 his Secret Self total and Blair Fate. Both numbers appear in every sector of his name.

The day number of his taking command was 2, his 'Life Path' number.

He was 44-years-old, a double 4 and, like the year number totalling 8, his Pulse number and Blair Persona number doubled up.

Labour party celebrate re-election 8 June 2001 (M-cycle 17. A-cycle 66. Personal Month 2).

8 6 2001
8 6 3
17
8

The M-cycle 17 denotes 8 like the day and date number. This is his Pulse Number.

The A-cycle is the master number 66, accentuating his 6 Fate and first name Persona number.

His Personal Month number 2 is the same as his Life Path.

The month number (June): 6. His Fate Number and Tony Persona.

The year number: 2001. Number 2 is his Life Path and number 1 is in his Secret Self Blair total, his full Fate Number and the full Fate Number for Tony.

He was 47 years old, which adds to 11/2 his Life Path.

The 'election' was conducted on the 7th June 2001, or 7 + 6 + 3, which totals 16, again both his numbers, as are the month and two numbers making up the year number. But, the presence of that 16 does not bode well for anyone who is abusing his position, taking the wrong path or lacking in integrity in some other way. From now on he would have to play a straight bat all the way down the wicket. We all know he didn't.

On 18th October 2003 his heart played up.
(M-cycle 18. A-cycle 69. Personal Month 6.)

18 10 2003
9 1 5
15
6

His M-cycle 18 is the same as the day number. This is composed of 1, his Persona total, his Blair Secret Self and his Tony Fate. And 8 his Pulse number.

His A-cycle 69 gives 6, as does the Personal Month and are his Tony Persona and full Fate number.

The month number 10/1 reflects his Persona total, his Blair Secret Self and his Tony Fate. The year number 5 agrees with his Secret Self and Blair Fate. Both numbers make up the date total 15.

On 1 October 2004 Tony Blair had a heart operation.
(M-cycle 18. A-cycle 70. Personal Month 5.)

1 10 2004
1 1 6
8

His M-cycle, 18 is the same as the date number. This is composed of 1, his Persona total, his Blair Secret Self and his Tony Fate. 8 is his Pulse number.

The A-cycle, 70 is a number of seeking wisdom, rest, retreat and resuscitation. 7 doesn't appear in Tony Blair's public name except as letter y, but it does in his full name in the Persona and doubled as 77 in his Secret Self.

His Personal Month is the same number as his Secret Self and Blair Fate.

The date total number 8 is his Pulse number.

The day and the month 10/1 agree with his Persona total, his Blair Secret Self and his Tony Fate. The year number 6 is the same as his birth day, Tony Persona, and Tony Blair Fate number. It also holds his Life Path number 2 and his Tony Secret Self and Blair Persona 4.

In 2004 the Blair's bought a house in London, it was number 29 of all things, 29 Connaught Square.

```
Secret Self number            1
                             10
                             19
                  10                   9
          6        1 3               3 1   5
       C o n n a u g h t   S q u a r e
          29     5 5       7 8 2   45 8       9
                  56                  62
                  11*                  8
                             19
                             10
Persona number                1
```

```
       C  o  n  n  a  u  g  h  t   S  q  u  a  r  e
      29  6  5  5  1  3  7  8  2  45  8  3  1  9  5
                66*                       71
                66*                        8
                             74
                             11*
Fate number                   2
```

Connaught:

A Secret Self number of 10 matches his Blair Secret Self, his full name Persona and his first name Fate.

A Persona number of 11/2 matches his Life Path.

A Fate (master number) 66 reflects his 6 full name Fate number, birth day and Tony Persona.

Square:

A Persona number of 62 includes 6, his full name Fate number, his birth day and his first name Persona. The 2 matches his Life Path.
The total Persona 8 is his Pulse number.
The Fate number 8 is his Pulse number.

The full interpretation of Connaught Square is just as fitting.

Connaught Square
Secret Self: 19/10/1
Persona: 19/10/1
Fate: 74/11/2

29 Connaught Square totals 29 + 74 = 103 = 1 + 0 + 3 = 4

or 11 (2 + 9) + 11 (7 + 4) = 22

Number 4 is Tony's Secret Self and the Blair Persona. The 2 of his Life Path is reflected in the 22.

London

Now let's have a look at the name 'London'.

The letter 'L' has a value of 38, but the sum of these numbers is 11, a *master number.*

Deciphering 'London' using 38

```
Secret Self               3
                           12
                        6     6
                      L o n d o n
                      38  5 4   5
                           52
Persona                   7

                      L o n d o n
                      38 6 5 4 6 5
                           64
                           10
Fate                      1
```

Deciphering London using its master number 11

```
Secret Self              3
                         12
                       6    6
                     L o n d o n
                     38  5 4   5
                     11  5 4   5
                    11    14
                    11     5
                         16
Persona                   7

                     L o n d o n
                     11 6 5 4 6 5
                    11    26
                    11     8
                         19
                         10
Fate                      1
```

Apart from the fact that ‘London’ contains every one of our *Tone’s* numbers what do the numbers have to tell us about London?

We can see that London’s numbers describe it well. It’s a seaport (52/7), it thinks of itself as a financial, fashion, literary, art and entertainment centre (3, 7, 8, 16 and 11); and it sees itself as a leader, and is the capital city (1 and 11) of Britain, the Commonwealth and the British Empire (but don’t tell anyone). An international judicial, martial and illuminist centre (8 and 11). It’s a busy (3) city (64) and international airport (3, 8 and 11) with an elitist, aloof personality (7, 8, 11). Runaways and fortune seekers flock to it (8, 11, 6 and 6). It has famous towers and hospitals (16) and has wrought and experienced tragic and dramatic activity (16). (It always will with these numbers.)

Because the capital letter L is a master number (11) appearing in the Persona sector this exaggerates any egocentric nature.

29 Connaught Square, London

29 Connaught Square, London totals 5, which is Tony Blair's Secret Self full name total and his Blair Fate total.

There'll be heartbreak here.

CHAPTER 7

Thoughts

One question, I suppose, is does Tony Blair have any idea of his numerological synchronicities and the drives these numbers have? Or did someone or something else? Can it really be just chance that all of his numbers are present in every major experience he has had? We mustn't lose sight of the fact that Tony Blair is not his real name. He was christened Anthony Charles Lynton Blair but his father's birth name was really Parsons. All of these names will be influencing him too. His name Anthony Charles Lynton Blair includes the same numbers as the name Tony Blair is motivated by, and more. And then what would the letters of Anthony Charles Lynton Parsons have to say?

Exactly the same numbers you'll find and all of them working in some mysterious way to account for every single number involved in all of the example events, and then all of the numbers related perfectly to the nature of the events themselves. That's the kicker.

At the time of writing, Tony Blair is reported to be in two minds whether to hold an election on 5th May 2005. He would be because a) He has a dual Life Path. b) The numbers, whilst they seem to be perfect for him, have lurking within them his Pulse number 8. The last election victory involved his Pulse number being drawn out of the bag and not long after he suffered heart problems, personal difficulties and exposure of his *truth economies*. And then there's the double 5. Could this mean that the power of the master 55 (5 and May) will trounce him, rather than propel him? The presence of number 5 in the year number doesn't help. In my view, if he goes for the election on this date he will not get the result he hopes for. There are two ways I can see this going if he goes for broke:

a) He'll lose or
b) Labour will win but someone else, probably Gordon Brown, will take the reins within the year (5 is also Gordon Brown's Secret Self and 8 his Fate number. He shares the same *Life Path* as Tony Blair being born on 20 February 1951, an 11/2 day).

But then who knows really what is on someone else's divinely ordained agenda? Even if what I propose comes true does that mean that numerology reveals the truth? Like everything we have at our disposal as physically bound beings we are limited by our perspective of something we have been alienated from. We might have known the Universal Unconscious prior to our conception but since then it has been flooded by very many thoughts, experiences and returning souls. It has moved on. Yet we are still inspired from this realm, some of us listen and some of us don't. And some of us communicate these understandings. Like many other writings, this book has manifested from just such a source. As has every single idea that has ever been. Every new idea comes when the conditions are right for it. New ideas don't always mean that the old ways were wrong. Often it may mean that they were inadequate for a curriculum we cannot yet perceive. We remain optimistic that we will continue to attain a progressive clarity. Individually and collectively we are all seeking the answer. The quest-i-on (little 'i'– not the ego 'I'), the quest i (*am*) on. And every one of those quests is uniquely tailored to each human spirit.

The essence or mind of every human being is dependent and connected to every other and numerology demonstrates this. We are all one, yet individual and everything that one of us does affects everyone else

Whether we like it or not, the matrix is the environment we live in. It seems constructed to impel us to meet myriad experiences incessantly creating, inflicting, gathering and transmitting sensations until we eventually jump off it and into the realm where spirit resides. There are only two choices – stay on it or get off. Choosing the latter will likely land you in another one, where you'll probably regret that you didn't stay in the game. And it is a game really, like Monopoly. Its rules are simple, do as much as you can with what life, (the die), throws at you; take your knocks, give everyone else a fair go, never cheat, and remain focussed. Play by the rules using your skills and discretion and get to the end having profited from the experience by as much as you can. And like Monopoly, in time everyone wins because there is always another game to play. It is another one of our blessings. Although the old folk may not have quite understood their advice to us when we were kids the wisdom of their words

"Count your blessings,' shines through. It is only now that I appreciate what they were saying. They were right god bless 'em.

And just one more thing to ponder…

Truth demands a pristine connection to the Source. No human being has that due to the reasons given in this book and more. It demands knowledge of everything. This deems every human judgement inept and is the meaning behind the biblical caution *'Judgement is mine sayeth the Lord!'*

Or perhaps we could consider it this way, if it can be explained it ain't true. But it could be truer…

Thank you for buying this book.

With Love,

www.biggyboo.com

Because I wanted to...

She danced a pretty ribbon song,

Entranced the boulder hard,
And eye gazed upon a secret whirled,
From twixt, between, becurl-ed,

What lies beneath your wails!
Vain citadel atop the rock,
Gleaming like sure-fire,

Do you know?

She yawned, that cavern deep,
Under that inkjet sky,
Or was it a smile... and wry?

No matter. We're Home, my friend Odie and I,

The hills and valleys,
The mountains and streams,
Then hark... my dog?...No! He dreams,

A voice... forlorn and sage-y,
T'was to my left,
And down... in a cleft,

'You are here,' he says,
'I sent for you.'

No!
I came because I wanted to.

Ellis

Inspired by Neil Hague's beautiful painting 'Cathar Portal',
the front cover illustration on this book.

Acknowledgements

Cover illustration from a painting by visionary artist, Neil Hague. Bless you mate, it's amazing!

Quotations from "As You Like It" and "Twelfth Night" both attributed to William Shakespeare

Thank you to Dawn, Fran P. and Mac for their proof reading and editing.

My thanks to the several hundred people from many 'walks of life' I met whilst giving private readings.

I was blessed by magnificent primary school teachers who stimulated my imagination and always encouraged me to think and to question, and to be. I guarantee no kid ever had better. To all of them who taught me at Blackbird Leys Primary School a great big thank you.

And last, but not least, thank you to every soul who has shone their light into my life, in whatever way. You have taught me so much more than I realised.

Ellis C Taylor no longer gives private consultations.

Ordering this book

U.K.

www.biggyboo.com

BiggyBoo Books
P.O. Box 23
Wheatley
Oxford
U.K.
OX33 1FL

U.S.A.

www.tgspublishing.com

Hidden Mysteries books
TGS Publishers
22241 Pinedale Lane
Frankston
Texas 75763
U.S.A.

903 876 3256

Months	1►
January - October	
October - July	*
July - April	
April - January	

Months	1►
February - November	
November - August	*
August - May	
May - February	

Months	1►
March - December	
December-September	*
September - June	
June - March	

Months	1►
April - January	
January - October	*
October - July	
July - April	

Months	1►
May - February	
February - November	*
November - August	
August - May	

Months	1►
June - March	
March - December	*
December-September	
September - June	

Months	1►
July - April	
April - January	*
January - October	
October - July	

Months	1►
August - May	
May - February	*
February - November	
November - August	

Months	1►
September - June	
June - March	*
March - December	
December-September	

Months	1►
October - July	
July - April	*
April - January	
January - October	

Months	1►
November - August	
August - May	*
May - February	
February - November	

Months	1►
December-September	
September - June	*
June - March	
March - December	

* The first month of this row is the birth month. Remember each cycle begins and ends on the birth day-number.

Other alphabet values

The French and German alphabets' letter values are the same as the English alphabet.

Below are the letter values for Italian.

Italian

Small letters

a	b	c	d	e	f	g	h	i	l	m*	n	o
1	2	3	4	5	6	7	8	9	10	11	12	13

p	q	r	s	t	u	v	z
14	15	16	17	18	19	20	21

Capital Letters

A*	B	C	D	E	F	G	H*	I	L	M	N*	O
22	23	24	25	26	27	28	29	30	31	32	33	34

P	Q	R	S*	T	U	V	Z
35	36	37	38	39	40	41	42

Master Letters: m, A, H, N, S

In modern numerology a letter value is determined by its numerical position in a given language's alphabet. Bear in mind that English is becoming the global language and its influence, especially in business, is steadily but surely over-riding every other.

Notes

Notes

Lightning Source UK Ltd.
Milton Keynes UK
UKHW022015130720
366473UK00008B/406